CW00643006

W

LITTLE BOOK OF LAUGHS

First published in Great Britain in 2010 by Prion
an imprint of the Carlton Publishing Group
20 Mortimer Street
London W1T 3JW

2 4 6 8 10 9 7 5 3 1

A catalogue record for this book is available from the British Library

ISBN 978-1-85375-771-6

Printed in China

THE WRINKLIES'

LITTLE BOOK OF LAUGHS

**By Mike Haskins
and Clive Whichelow**

PRION

INTRODUCTION

Welcome, wrinkly laugh-lovers, to
this little book of fun. I just hope they
used a nice big font so you won't have
to use your glasses. I did ask, mind
you, people seem to take less notice
these days…

MIKE 'N' CLIVE

As we grow older year by year, my husband always mourns: the less and less we feel our oats, the more we feel our corns.

Have you ever thought, in 40 years' time when they're going over all the things they had to do without when they were young, what exactly are the children of today going to moan about?

An old man is being shown round a house by an estate agent. "This house," says the estate agent, "is not only beautifully appointed and in first class decorative order, but it's a fabulous long-term investment." "Long-term?" says the old man. "You're joking aren't you? Blimey, at my time of life I don't even buy green bananas!"

Everyone is sitting in their seats at the theatre waiting for the performance to start when suddenly a middle-aged woman at the back of the stalls stands up and shouts, "Is there a doctor in the house?" Five men stand up and the woman says, "Thank goodness for that, now if any of you are single would you like to marry my beautiful daughter?"

One day someone suddenly realizes that your eldest child is almost 40, which puts you at 56 at the absolute minimum and more likely well into your 60s. It's at this point that you quickly say, "Look, I've never told him, but he was adopted." Just don't over-egg it by trying to pretend that he was 32 when you took him on.

A doctor begins his examination of an old man by asking him what brought him to the hospital. "Er," says the old man. "I think it might have been an ambulance."

You Know You're Getting Old When... You come out of a supermarket and spend 15 minutes looking for your car before remembering you gave up driving four years ago.

An old man goes to see his doctor. "Well," says the doctor, "it's a long time since you've been to see me." "I know," says the old man, "I've not been well."

For a long time old Tom's family thought he had become hunchbacked due to his advancing years. Eventually, though, they found out that it was just because he didn't know his braces were adjustable.

A lady in her late 80s goes to the doctor's for a check-up. The doctor asks her how she's doing and receives in response a litany of complaints about her aches, pains, stiffness, lack of energy and her general increasing difficulty at doing many things. "Now come on, Mrs Siegel," says the doctor. "You have to expect things to start deteriorating at your age. After all, who wants to live to be 100?" The old lady gives him a cold look and replies, "I would have thought anyone who's 99."

A man is at the doctors to hear the results of his tests. "Well, doctor," he says, "is it good news or bad news?" "Bad news I'm afraid," replies the doctor. "You've only got three months to live." "Three months!" exclaims the patient. "Is there nothing I can do?" "Well, you could try having lots of mud baths," says the doctor. "And that'll prolong my life will it?" asks the patient hopefully. "No," replies the doctor, "but at least it'll get you used to lying in dirt."

Tom, Dick and Harry are three old friends. Tom is 80, Dick is 90 and Harry is 100 years old. They all go to the doctor's together for a check-up. Tom goes in first and comes out a few minutes later and tells the others, "The doctor says I'm in extremely good health for an 80-year-old. He thinks I could live another 20 years." Dick goes into the consulting room next and emerges a little while later. He tells the others, "The doctor says I'm in fairly good health considering the fact that I'm 90. He says I could live for another ten years." Harry goes in last and comes out an hour later. "What happened?" ask his friends. "The doctor examined me and then asked how old I was," says Harry. "And what happened when you told him?" asks Tom. "He told me to have a nice day," says Harry.

An old man goes to the doctor and says he hasn't been feeling well. The doctor gives him an examination, and then goes to his cupboard and brings out three large bottles of different coloured pills. "Now then," says the doctor, "I want you to take the green pill with a big glass of water when you get out of bed. Then I want you to take the blue pill with a big glass of water after your dinner. Then just before you go to bed, I want you to take the red pill with another big glass of water." The old man is surprised

that the doctor wants to put him on
so much medication so he says, "So,
doctor, exactly what it is that I've got
wrong with me?" "You're not drinking
enough water," says the doctor.

While it may not be entirely true to
say that all the people who live in
Bournemouth are getting on a bit, it is
one of the few places where the shops
on the high street have to have their
windows made from bifocal lenses.

A pharmacist is going over the directions on a prescription bottle with an elderly patient. "Be sure not to take this more often than every four hours," the pharmacist says. "Don't worry about that," replies the patient. "It takes me four hours to get the bloomin' lid off!"

A middle-aged man is due to have an operation and is very worried about it, so just beforehand he tells the surgeon that he's rather nervous and concerned. "You see, doctor," he says, "I've heard that only one in ten people survives this particular operation. Is that true?" "Unfortunately, yes," admits the surgeon. "Your information is correct. But looking on the bright side you've got absolutely nothing to worry about because my last nine patients all died!"

Two ageing nuns are talking about where they should go for their holidays. Sister Teresa has gone a bit deaf so Sister Rita has to use hand gestures in order to communicate. "I'd like to go to Florida," says Sister Rita. "You know! Florida! Where the oranges are this big and the bananas are this long." In the end Sister Teresa speaks very slowly, with very exaggerated hand gestures. "Florida!" she says. "Where the oranges are THIS BIG and the bananas are THIS LONG." "Which priest are you talking about again?" asks Sister Teresa.

A very old man, almost bent double, hobbles up to an ice-cream seller and asks for a vanilla cornet. "Crushed nuts, granddad?" asks the ice-cream man. "No," says the old man. "It's rheumatism if you must know."

At a nursing home, a group of senior citizens is sitting around talking about their aches and pains. "My arms are so weak I can hardly lift this cup of coffee," says one. "I know what you mean," says another. "My cataracts are so bad I can't even see my coffee." "I've got all those problems," says another member of the group, "plus my blood pressure pills make me dizzy all the time. I suppose that's the price we pay for getting old." The group sits silently for a few moments before an old lady pipes up. "Look on the bright side," she says. "At least we're all still able to drive."

An old man goes to the doctor's for an examination. On his way out of the surgery he has a heart attack and drops dead on the spot. The doctor leaps into action and tells the receptionist, "Quick! Turn him round and make it look like he was just walking in."

Two old ladies are talking one day. One says to the other, "Even though I'm 75 men still look at my boobs." "Oh yes," says the second. "I bet they have to squat down a bit first though."

An old man tells his friend, "Despite her age, my wife really doesn't seem to be growing old gracefully. Last week she took part in a wet shawl contest."

Three old men are at the doctor's to have their memories tested. The doctor says to the first old man, "What's 3 times 3?" "274," is his reply. The doctor worriedly says to the second old man, "It's your turn. What's 3 times 3?" "Tuesday," replies the second old man. The doctor sadly says to the third old man, "OK, it's your turn. What's 3 times 3?" "Nine," says the third old man. "Excellent!" exclaims the doctor. "How did you get that?" "Oh come on, doctor. That was simple," says the old man. "I just subtracted 274 from Tuesday."

Agnes is celebrating her hundredth birthday and the local paper sends round a young reporter to interview her. "So, Mrs Ellis," he says, "what do you put your long life down to?" "Well," replies the old lady, "I think a bit of what you fancy does you good. I've always eaten in moderation, and I've drunk in moderation, and hardly ever smoked, and I've always done gentle exercise." "I see," says the reporter, "But your daughter tells me you've often been bedridden." "Of course I have," says Agnes. "Repeatedly. But don't put that in your flipping newspaper, will you?"

An old lady decides her body has got out of shape, so she joins a fitness club to do some exercise. She signs on to do an aerobics class for senior citizens. On her first day she bends, twists, gyrates, jumps up and down, and perspires for an hour. But, by the time she manages to get her leotard on, the class has finished.

An old man is a witness in a burglary case. The defence lawyer asks him, "Did you see my client commit this burglary?" "Oh yes," says the old man. "But this crime took place at night," says the lawyer. "Are you sure you saw my client commit this crime?" "Yes," says the old man, "I saw him do it." So the lawyer says to the old man, "Sir, you are an elderly man now over 80 years old. Are you really going to tell this court that your eyesight was good enough for you to see my client from several feet away? Just how far do you think you are able to see at night?" "Well," says the old man, "I can see the moon. How far is that?"

Two old women are chatting over coffee one morning and Mildred says, "How's your husband doing in the bedroom department these days?" Ethel replies, "Ooh, Mildred, I tell you what, he makes me feel like an exercise bike. Every day he climbs on and starts pumping away, but we never seem to get anywhere."

Old John decides to start doing some exercise to get his weight down so he joins his local health club and has a go on the running machine. He does very well on his first day and manages to lose one and a half stone. Unfortunately he manages this because the machine tears his leg off.

Old Tom used to swear by a glass of liver salts. He used to drink a glass after every meal, every single day of his life. Finally he died at the grand old age of 95 and at the funeral the mourners had to beat his liver to death with a stick.

A vicar goes to visit a little old lady who lives in his parish. She shows him into her living room and there sitting on a perch is her pet parrot. "I can't help noticing," says the vicar, "that you seem to have tied a ribbon to each of your parrot's legs. What are they for?" "Well," says the old lady, "If I pull the left ribbon he sings 'Abide With Me' and if I pull on the right ribbon he sings 'All Things Bright and Beautiful'." "Oh my goodness!" chuckles the vicar. "I wonder, though, what happens if you pull both ribbons at the same time?" "I fall off the flipping perch, you idiot," says the parrot.

An old lady orders a new carpet for her living room and a man turns up to fit it for her. After he's put the carpet down, the man feels in his pocket for his packet of cigarettes and finds they're missing. He then notices a lump in the middle of the old lady's new carpet. "Oh no!" he says to himself, "I've dropped my fags and laid the carpet on top of them." In the end he decides the easiest thing is to get a hammer and gently tap the lump until it's completely flat. Just as he's got the bulge level, the old lady walks in with his pack of cigarettes in her hand. "Look!" she says, "You must have dropped these in the hall. Now I wonder if you could help me to find something. My pet budgie seems to have gone missing somewhere..."

An old lady receives a computer for her birthday. Her son tells her he is keen to teach her the advantages of the World Wide Web. He sets up the computer and sits his mother down in front of it. He demonstrates how to switch it on, how to access the internet and how to search for information. "I'm not sure about this," says the old lady. "It's easy, Mum," says her son. "Just pretend the search engine is a person you're talking to. Just ask it a question, press return and it'll answer anything you want." The old lady reaches for the keyboard and types into Google: "Hello. How are Auntie Ginnie's varicose veins?"

Two ageing ladies are talking in the beauty parlour one day. "Of course I've always had a nice firm chin," says one. "Yes," says the other one, "in fact now I see the firm has taken on a couple of partners."

A husband and wife are getting ready for bed. The wife is standing in front of a full-length mirror, taking a long hard look at herself. "You know dear," she says, "I look in the mirror and I see an old woman. My face is all wrinkled, my hair is grey, my shoulders are hunched over, I've got fat legs and my arms are flabby." She turns to her husband and says, "Tell me something positive, to make me feel better about myself." He studies hard for a moment, and says "Well, there's nothing wrong with your eyesight."

A middle-aged woman goes off to a health centre for a week and has a series of beauty treatments, including waxing, facials, a special diet, saunas and more. When she gets back home, fully revitalized and glowing with health, she asks her husband, "So, if you'd never met me before, just on the way I look now, how old would you say I was?" Her husband looks her up and down and says, "I'd say from your skin, 26. From your hair about 20. And from your body..." The woman giggles girlishly and says,

"You old flatterer, don't you think you're overdoing it a bit?" "Hold on," says the husband, "I haven't added them up yet."

A 60-year-old man decides to have a face-lift for his birthday. He spends £10,000 and is really happy with the results. On his way home, he stops at a newsagent and buys a paper. While he's there, he asks the sales assistant, "I hope you don't mind me asking, but how old do you think I am?" "About 40," says the sales assistant. "I'm actually 60," says the man feeling very pleased with himself. After that, he goes into a chip shop for some lunch and asks the assistant there the same question. The assistant says, "I'd say about 35." "Thanks very much," says the man, "I'm actually 60." Later, while he's waiting at a bus stop, he asks an old woman the same question. She replies, "I'm 85 years old, and my eyesight is going. But if I have a feel in your pants, I will be able to tell." As there is no-one around, the man lets her slip her hand down his pants. Ten minutes later, the old lady says, "Right. You're 60 years old." "That's incredible," says the man, "You're exactly right. How do you do that?" "I was behind you in the chip shop," says the old lady.

Edna is a 45-year-old woman. One day she has a heart attack and is taken to hospital. While on the operating table she has a near-death experience. Seeing God she asks, "Is this it? Is my time up?" God replies, "No, Edna, my child. You have come here too soon. In fact you have another 43 years, two months and eight days to live." Upon recovery, Edna decides to stay in the hospital and have a face-lift, liposuction, breast implants and a tummy tuck. She even has someone come in and change her hair colour and brighten her teeth!

Well, she thinks to herself, I may as well make the most of it. Afterwards, she gets out of hospital but, while crossing the street on her way home, she is run over by an ambulance and killed. She arrives up in Heaven in front of God and is completely furious. "What's going on?" she asks God. "I thought you said I had another 43 years? Why didn't you pull me from out of the path of the ambulance?" "Oh, sorry, Edna," replies God, "I didn't recognize you!"

An old man is trying to get his reluctant old friend to come out for a walk. "What happened to your get up and go," he asks. "It got up and went without me," says his friend.

A man tells his friend, "My wife went in for a face-lift operation last week." "Did it work?" asks the friend. "Not really," says the man. "When they saw what was under it, they dropped it again."

An old couple arrive at the airport just in the nick of time to catch the plane for their summer holiday. "Do you know what?" says the old lady, "I wish I'd brought the piano with us." "What on earth are you talking about?" says her husband, "Why would you want to bring the piano with you?" "Because," says the old lady, "I've left our tickets on top of it."

A newspaper reporter visits a very old man on his birthday. "Have you lived in this town your whole life?" asks the reporter. "Obviously not, you young fool," says the old man. "I haven't died yet, have I?"

A man goes to a reunion of all his old classmates from school. The next day his friend asks him how it went. "It was OK," he says, "but unfortunately all my old friends had become so old and overweight, hardly any of them seemed to recognize me."

At the seaside there are two old men on their annual holiday standing in the sea with their trousers rolled up, smoking their pipes and watching the boats go by. One of them glances down at the other one's feet and says, "Blimey, mate, look at the state of your feet, they're absolutely filthy!" The other one looks down and agrees. "Yeah, I know," he says, "we couldn't come last year."

A lbert and Henry are taking a stroll along the sea front one day when a seagull flies over and drops a blob of excrement right on the top of Albert's bald head. Henry is horrified at what has just happened and says in great concern, "Wait right there. I'll be back in a moment." Henry waddles off as fast as he can go to the nearest public convenience and returns a few minutes later with a length of toilet paper. "It's a bit too late for that," says Albert. "That seagull will be miles away by now."

A plane has a rough flight over the ocean. Suddenly a voice comes over the intercom: "Ladies and gentlemen, please fasten your seat belts and assume crash positions. We have lost our engines and we are trying to put this baby down as gently as possible on the water." "Oh stewardess! Are there any sharks in the ocean below?" asks a little old lady, terrified. "Yes, I'm afraid there are some. But not to worry, we have a special gel in the bottle next to your chair designed especially for emergencies like this. Just rub the gel onto your arms and legs." "And if I do this, the sharks won't eat me any more?" asks the lady. "Oh, they'll eat you all right, only they won't enjoy it so much," answers the stewardess.

An old lady decides one day that she really should learn to drive. So after many attempts she passes her test and tells her husband that to celebrate she's going to drive him over to France for a holiday. But then a week before the trip she suddenly announces the holiday is off. "Why did you change your mind?" he asks. "Well," says the old lady, "it's this business of driving on the right. I've been practising round town for three weeks now and I just can't get used to it – in fact, I've nearly killed three people."

A police officer is driving along one day when he sees an old lady in her car, driving along while knitting at the same time. The police man attempts unsuccessfully to get her attention, but to no avail. Finally he drives right alongside her, winds down his window and calls out, "Pull over, madam!" At which points the old lady turns to him and says, "No. Socks actually."

A rich old man goes to a dating agency and ends up going to have dinner with an elderly dowager. The next day at his London club a friend asks him if he enjoyed himself. "Well," says the old man, "I would have done if the melon had been as cold as the soup, and the soup had been as warm as the wine, and the wine had been as old as the chicken, and if the chicken had been as young as the maid, and the maid had been as willing as the old dowager then, yes, I would have had a very good time indeed."

Two old ladies were sitting in the park enjoying some music. "I think it's a minuet from Mignon," said one. "I thought it was a waltz from Faust," said the other. So the first old lady got up and shuffled over to a nearby notice board. "We were both wrong," she said. "It's a Refrain from Spitting."

A wealthy old dowager goes to the National Gallery one day and tries to impress one of the attendants. "Oh, look!" she says, "A Goya." "Er, no, madam, it's a Gainsborough," corrects the attendant. "Ah," says the old woman, "but that one… definitely a Renoir." "A Seurat," says the attendant. "Oh," says the woman, glancing around hastily to find one she definitely knows. "Now that horrible, ugly scary-looking one; I know that for certain. It's *The Scream* by Edvard Munch." "No, madam," says the attendant. "That is in fact a mirror."

Two old ladies are visiting an art gallery one day and walk through the sculpture section. A few minutes later they emerge looking rather shocked and shaken. "Blimey!" says the first one. "Did you see that statue of that feller?" "What, the feller with the big doodah hanging out for everyone to see?" says her friend. "Yes I did see that. Absolutely enormous wasn't it?" "I know," says the first one, "and it was so cold in that art gallery as well."

An elderly man bought a large farm in Florida and fixed it up with walkways, orchards, tennis courts and a pond at the furthest edge of the property. One evening he decided to go down to the pond and took a bucket with him to bring back some fruit. As he got nearer, he heard voices shouting and laughing with glee. As he came closer he saw a bunch of young women skinny-dipping in his pond. He made the women aware of his presence and they all went into the deep end. One of the women shouted to him,

"Hey, you old pervert! We're not coming out of here until you leave!" "That's OK," said the old man, "I didn't come down here to watch you ladies swim naked or make you get out of the pond naked." Then he held up his bucket and said, "I'm just here to feed my alligator!"

One night an old woman is horrified to see a police car pull up outside her house, even more so when she sees her husband brought out of the back and led up to the door. "What happened?" the old lady asks the policeman. "I'm sorry, madam," says the policeman, "We found this elderly gentleman at the local shopping centre. He was lost and couldn't remember how to get home." "Oh no!" says the old woman. After the police have gone she turns to her husband and says, "The shopping centre's only half a mile away. How could you have forgotten your way home? You're not losing your marbles are you?" "Of course not," says her old husband. "I wasn't lost. I was just too tired to walk."

An old man goes up to a young man at the post office and says, "Excuse me, would you address this postcard for me?" The young man gladly does so and then says, "Would you like me to write a short message on here for you as well?" "Yes, please," says the old man and dictates what he would like to say. Finally the young man, feeling very pleased with himself for his good deed, asks, "Now, is there anything else I can do for you?" The old man thinks a moment and says, "Yes, please. At the end could you just add, 'Please excuse the sloppy handwriting.'"

A rambler in the country sees an old farmer sitting on his porch, holding a small length of rope and studying it intently. "Good afternoon," says the rambler, "What's the rope for?" "I use it to tell the weather," says the old farmer. "Really?" says the rambler, impressed. "How does it work?" "Well," says the farmer, "When the rope shifts slightly from side to side, that means it's windy. And when it feels wet, that means it's raining."

An old Cherokee chief sat in his reservation hut, smoking a ceremonial pipe, eyeing the two US government officials sent to interview him. "Chief Two Eagles," one official began, "you have observed the white man for many generations, you have seen his wars and his products, you have seen all his progress and all his problems." The chief nodded. The official continued, "Considering recent events, in your opinion, where has the white man gone wrong?" The chief stared at the government officials for

over a minute and then calmly replied:
"When white man found the land,
Indians were running it. No taxes.
No debt. Plenty buffalo. Plenty beaver.
Women did the work. Medicine man
free. Indian men hunted and fished
all the time." The chief smiled and
added quietly, "White man dumb
enough to think he could improve
system like that."

An 80-year-old man is having a check-up at the doctor's. As the doctor listens to the man's heart, he mutters, "Uh oh!" "What's the problem?" asks the old man. "Well," says the doctor, "you have a serious heart murmur. Do you smoke?" "No," says the old man. "Are you a heavy drinker?" asks the doctor. "No," says the man. "Do you have much of a sex life?" asks the doctor. "Yes," says the old man, "That's my sole remaining pleasure in life." "OK," says the doctor, "but now you've got this heart murmur, you're going to have to give up half your sex life." "OK," says the old man, "but which half do you want me to give up? The looking or the thinking?"

The old farmer and his wife are getting ready for their 50th wedding anniversary dinner. The farmer's wife says, "Albert, should I go out in the yard and kill a chicken?" Albert says, "Oh come on Phyllis, why blame a chicken for something that happened 50 years ago?"

Bryan says to Dave, "It's your 20th wedding anniversary soon, isn't it, Dave? What are you going to buy the missus?" "A once-in-a-lifetime trip to Australia," says Dave. "Wow!" says Bryan. "I'm sure she'll be absolutely thrilled, but how on earth will you top that on your 25th anniversary?" "Well," says Dave, "I was thinking maybe then I could send her the money to pay for her ticket back."

An old couple have gone back to their honeymoon hotel every year on their wedding anniversary. One year, when they're shown to their room, they find they've been given a whole suite rather than the usual double room. "Excuse me," says the old man to the hotel porter. "I think there's been a mistake. This is the bridal suite." "That's all right sir," says the porter. "There's no need to perform. If we'd put you in the kitchen we wouldn't be expecting you to knock up dinner."

J oe says to Pete, "On our silver wedding anniversary the wife and I went back to the same little country hotel where we spent our wedding night." "And was it all just the same?" asks Pete. "Almost," says Joe, "except this time I was the one crying my heart out in the bathroom."

Two old men are looking round a National Trust property when one says to the other, "You know, visiting these historical sites isn't so much fun when they all turn out to be younger than you are."

Two old men are talking over some sad memories. "You know it's 40 years today I lost my wife and children," says one. "Is it really?" says the other. "That's terrible." "Yes it is," says the first. "I'll never forget that poker game."

On their 30th wedding anniversary a couple go back to the resort where they spent their honeymoon. On the way, they are driving through the countryside when the man says, "Look! Remember that field? Remember what we did on the way to our hotel 30 years ago?" The wife smiles and says, "Oh yes!" So they get out of the car and make love right up against the wire fence. When they get back in the car the husband says, "Wow! That was amazing! You were even more animated than 30 years ago!" "I know I was," says the wife, "because 30 years ago that bloomin' fence wasn't electrified!"

A married couple are celebrating their 60th wedding anniversary. At the party everybody wants to know how they've managed to stay together so long in this day and age. The husband tells them, "When we were first married we came to an agreement. I would make all the major decisions and my wife would make all the minor decisions. Well, can you believe it? I'm able to tell you today that in 60 long years of marriage, we've never needed to make a single major decision."

Every week, in church, the vicar notices one old couple who are always sitting in the same pew holding hands. Thinking that at their age this is rather charming he stops them one week on their way out to remark on it. "I can't help noticing," says the vicar, "how close you both seem even after all these years, holding hands and so on." "Close! Don't be so ridiculous!" says the old woman. "I'm just trying to stop the old bugger cracking his knuckles all the way through the service!"

A couple are celebrating their 40th wedding anniversary. A friend asks them, "What's your secret for such a long marriage?" "We take the time to go out to a restaurant twice a week," says the husband. "You know the sort of thing. A candlelight dinner, soft music and a slow walk home." "That's lovely," says the friend. "Yes it is," says the husband. "My wife goes on Tuesdays and I go on Fridays."

A 60-year-old couple are celebrating their 40th wedding anniversary. During the celebration a fairy appears and says that, since they've been such a loving couple, she'll give them each one wish. The wife wishes to travel around the world. The fairy waves her wand and poof! She has a handful of plane tickets. Next, it's the husband's turn. He pauses for a moment, then says, "I'd like to have a woman 30 years younger than me." So the fairy picks up her wand and poof! He's 90!

A married couple have been together for years. One night the husband is reading the newspaper when his wife tells him, "I wish I was your newspaper. Then you'd give me your full attention for hours every evening." "Oh that's nice, darling," says the man. "You know I wish I could have a wife like a newspaper as well." "Oh yes," says the woman. "Because then you'd be able to put your hands all over me every night?" "No," says the husband. "Because then I could throw the old one out each night and pick up a nice, fresh, new one every morning."

On their 40th wedding anniversary a man says to his wife, "Whatever you want, just name it and I'll buy it for you. It doesn't matter how much it costs. Just say what you'd like for our anniversary." She replies, "A divorce." "To be honest," he says. "I wasn't thinking of spending quite that much."

Old Alf is 80 years old when he marries a 20-year-old woman and after a few months she is pregnant. "Are you sure this is a good idea?" Alf's doctor asks him. "It seems a bit late in life to be having another child." "I think it's the perfect time for me to have a baby," says old Alf. "After all I have to get up 12 times during the night now anyway!"

An ageing man marries a beautiful young bride many years his junior. On their honeymoon night they climb into bed and the old man asks his new bride, "Tell me, did your mother tell you what to do on your wedding night?" "Oh yes," she says. "She told me everything I needed to know." "That's handy," says the elderly gentleman as he turns out the light. "Because I seem to have forgotten."

An old farmer gets married to an 18-year-old. A few weeks after the service, the vicar decides to call round at the farm to ask the old boy how things are going with his new young wife. "Oh," says the old man, "I can't keep my hands off her." The vicar mumbles his approval and goes on his way. A few weeks later he calls round again and asks the same question. "I still can't keep my hands off her," says the old man. "I suppose that's good," says the vicar. "Not really," says the old farmer. "She's gone and run off with one of them."

An ageing multi-millionaire gets married to a beautiful 19-year-old model. His friend tells him, "You're an old devil. How did you manage to marry a beautiful young girl like that when you're 60?" "It was partly the money," says the old man, "and partly the fact that I told her I was 95."

A feminist woman gets on a bus one day and all the seats are taken, so an old man stands up. "No thank you!" says the woman, pushing him back in his seat. "The world has moved on." At the next stop a woman gets on and again the old man stands up. Now angry, the feminist pushes him back down. "We don't need your patronising gestures!" she fumes. At the next stop a third woman gets on and again the old man stands up. "You just don't get it, do you, granddad?" screams the woman. Now it's the old man's turn to be angry, "Look, you old boiler, just let me off the bloody bus will you! I've missed three stops already!"

An old couple are sitting at the dinner table when the old man sneezes very loudly. "Well," says the old woman, "I notice that you've finally learnt some manners and have started to put your hand in front of your mouth when you sneeze." "I have to, don't I?" says the old man. "It's the only way I can catch my teeth."

A reporter asks a rich old American man how he made his money. The old man replies, "Well, son, it was 1932. The depth of the Great Depression. I was down to my last nickel and I invested that nickel in an apple. I spent the entire day polishing the apple and, at the end of the day, I sold that apple for ten cents. The next morning, I invested those ten cents in two apples. I spent the entire day polishing them and sold them for 20 cents. I continued this system for a month, by the end of which I'd accumulated a fortune of $1.37. Then my wife's father died and left us two million dollars."

An ageing human cannonball goes to tell the circus ringmaster that, after 50 years in the job, he feels he's had enough and he wants to retire after tonight's performance. "Oh no," says the ringmaster, begging him to reconsider. "Where else will I find a man of your calibre?"

A pretty young girl walks up to the fabric counter in a large department store and says, "I want to buy some material for a new dress. How much does it cost?" "To a pretty little thing like you, miss," says the male assistant, "it's one kiss per yard." "OK," says the girl. "I'll take ten yards." With expectation and anticipation written all over his face, the clerk hurriedly measures out and wraps the cloth, then holds it out teasingly. The girl snatches the package. "Thanks," she says and points to a little old man standing beside her. "My granddad will pay."

An old people's home gets a celebrity visit from Cliff Richard. Cliff arrives and before he leads them all in a sing-along, he goes round saying hello to all the elderly residents. Unfortunately no-one seems to recognise him, so Cliff says to one old lady, "What about you? Do you have any idea who I am?" "No, sorry, dear," says the old lady. "But let's call one of the nurses over. I'm sure they'll be able to tell you."

The old people's home next gets a special visit from Bruce Forsyth. Bruce tells the residents a series of funny jokes and they all seem to find his act extremely amusing. Afterwards Bruce says to the matron, "That seemed to go well, dear. A couple of the audience laughed so much they wet themselves." "Don't kid yourself, Bruce," says the matron, "they'd have done that whether you were here or not."

A man finds a place for his elderly mother at a care home. All the residents are given a wristband on which can be written details of any food allergies they have. Unfortunately the man is not told about this and, when he comes to visit his mother the next day, he is furious when he finds the staff have stuck a wrist band on her on which is written the single word, 'Bananas'.

Two very old men are sitting outside the Sunnyglades rest home watching the world go by when one asks the other how he's feeling today. "Oh," he says, "do you know what, I feel just like a little baby." "What happy and healthy and full of energy?" "No," says the other one, "bald and toothless, and I think I've just filled my nappy."

A charity organized a special Christmas lunch for elderly people. A couple of weeks after the event they received a thank you letter. It said: "I am just writing to thank you for your Christmas lunch, where I was lucky enough to win a lovely portable radio in the raffle. In my retirement home I share a room with another elderly lady who would occasionally allow me to listen to her radio when she was feeling generous, until it broke recently. Now I have my own radio and when she asks if she can listen to it I can say, 'No, you can't you old cow!'"

The manager of an old people's home decides to hire an animal act to entertain everyone at the home's annual tea-party. He calls a theatrical agent. "I've got a tiger," says the agent. "It does a high wire act and juggles plates." "Too dangerous!" replies the manager. "It might fall on someone or bite them. What we need is something unusual, but sedate, so it won't upset them." "I know," says the agent. "How about Morris the gibbon? He's very quiet. All he does is card tricks." "Perfect," replies the manager. "Let's try a mellow gibbon round the old folk's tea..."

An old man and an old woman decide to get married. As part of the preparations, they visit their local chemist's shop. Inside the old man asks the chemist, "Tell me, do you supply a range of heart medicines here?" "Oh yes," says the chemist. "What about vitamin supplements?" asks the old man. "Of course," says the chemist. "Lumbago ointment?" "Yes." "Pills for arthritis." "Yes." "Viagra." "Yes." "Incontinence pants." "Yes." "Excellent," says the old man, "Darling, I think we've found just the place to do our wedding list."

An 85-year-old widow goes out on a blind date with a 90-year-old man. When she gets home later that night, she seems to be rather upset. "What happened?" asks her daughter. "Oh it was terrible," says the old widow. "I had to slap that man's face three times." "Oh no," says the daughter. "You don't mean he got fresh with you?" "I wish he had," says the old widow. "No, I kept thinking he was dead."

Old Bert falls in love with old Ethel and decides to propose. As a stickler for tradition, Bert takes Ethel's hand, gets down on one knee and tells her there are two things he would like to ask her. "What's the first?" asks Ethel. "Will you marry me?" says old Bert. "Oh yes," says Ethel. "What's the second?" "Can you help me back up?" says Bert.

An old couple are sitting on their sofa watching television one night. During one of the commercial breaks, the old woman asks, "Whatever happened to our sexual relations?" After a long thoughtful silence, her slightly deaf husband replies, "I don't know. We didn't even get a Christmas card from them last year did we?"

An old couple are sitting in the local park on a beautiful spring day. "Spring days like this really take me back," says the husband. "Do they?" says his wife. "Tell me, do you remember the first time we ever made love?" The old man sits and thinks for a moment and then says, "No. In fact to be honest with you, I can't remember the last time."

Two old soldiers are watching young girls walk by in the park one day when one says to the other, "You remember how when we were young servicemen, they used to put Bromide in our tea to stop us thinking about girls." "Yes," says his friend. "Well," says the first, "I think mine's finally begun to work."

An old man was passing a group of giggling teenagers in the park. "What's the joke, lads?" asked the old man. "Oh nothing," said one boy, "We were just seeing who could tell the biggest lie about their sex life." "You young boys just disgust me!" exclaimed the old man. "Do you know, when I was your age, I never even thought about sex." After a pause the boys all cried in unison, "OK, granddad! You win!"

One afternoon, an elderly couple are relaxing in front of the television. Suddenly, the woman is overcome with lust and says to her husband, "Let's go upstairs and make love." "Which would you prefer?" asks her elderly husband. "I'm not sure I can do both."

An old man shuffles very slowly into the doctor's surgery and says, "Doctor, I need you to give me something to lower my sex drive." "How old are you?" asks the doctor. "Ninety-six," says the man. "Ninety-six and you want to lower your sex drive!" says the doctor. "I would have thought at your age, it's all in your head." "It is," says the old man. "That's why I want you to lower it."

Three middle-aged women are talking about their love lives. Daphne says, "My husband is like a Rolls-Royce convertible; smooth, sleek and sophisticated." Beryl says, "Mine is like a Ferrari. Fast, furious and incredibly powerful." Blanche, the oldest one of the group, says, "Mine's like an old Morris Minor. Needs a hand start and you have to jump on quick once you've got it going."

A senior citizen shuffles painfully into a house of ill repute and asks how much it will cost him for a night of pleasure. "Two hundred pounds," replies the madam. "Two hundred pounds!" splutters the old man. "Are you putting me on?" "We can if you want," says the madam, "but that will be an extra ten quid."

An elderly man hobbles into a brothel and tells the madam he would like a young girl for the night. Surprised, she looks at the ancient wizened creature and asks how old he is. "I'm 90 years old," gasps the old fellow. "Ninety years old!" replies the madam. "Sorry, pop. I think you've had it." "Oh, have I?" says the old man, fumbling for his wallet. "So how much do I owe you?"

One evening in the retirement home 90-year-old Elsie came downstairs in a see-through negligee and approached three old men sitting on the sofa. "Now then, boys," she announced, holding up a clenched fist, "whoever can guess what I'm holding in my hand gets to spend the night with me, making wild passionate love!" "An elephant?" suggested one appalled old man. "That's close enough, dearie!" she said, grabbing him by the hand and leading him away.

Two old widows in their 80s are sitting in their chairs in their retirement home. "Tell me," says one to the other, "when you were married, did you and your husband have mutual orgasms?" The second old widow thinks for a few moments and then says, "No, I think we were with the Prudential."

A little old lady walks into a police station. "I want to report something, officer," she tells the desk sergeant. "I was walking through the park when a great big beast of a man leapt out of the bushes and molested me all over my body." "Oh yes," says the policeman, "and did this happen this morning?" "No," says the old lady. "It was in 1957." "That's quite a long time ago," says the policeman, "Why are you telling me about it now?" "Oh, you know," says the old lady, "it's nice just to reminisce occasionally."

An old maid gets held up in a dark alley. She says she has no money on her, but the robber insists that she's lying and that she's got her cash hidden somewhere about her person. He then starts feeling all over her trying to find the money. After a few minutes of squeezing and fiddling with every bit of her body, the old lady says, "I told you, young man, I haven't got any money. But... ooo-er... if you keep doing that I could always write you a cheque!"

Three little old ladies are sitting on a park bench when a man in a raincoat jumps out from a bush and flashes them. Two of the women have a stroke, but the other one can't quite reach.

Two old dears go to the zoo and visit the elephants' enclosure. One male elephant seems to be in a bad mood and is rampaging around with a large erection. "Oh my goodness!" says Ethel. "Do you think he'll charge?" Her friend replies, "By the look of him, love, I think he'd be entitled to, don't you?"

Two old men are sitting in the garden of a home for retired gentle folk. Suddenly one of the elderly female residents runs past them, streaking. "My goodness!" says the first. "Wasn't that Elsie Clitheroe?" "I think it was," says his friend. "She's 98, you know," says the first. "Yes," says the other. "What was that she was wearing?" "I don't know," says his companion. "But it looked like it could do with a good iron."

An old couple are sitting at home one day when the old lady asks her husband, "So, granddad are you going to take any of those Viagra tablets I got for you?" The old man looks at her and says, "No, I'm not." "Why not?" asks the old lady. "Because," says the old man, "there's no point putting lead in your pencil if you haven't got anyone worth writing to."

An elderly man goes to his chemist and asks for Viagra. "OK," says the pharmacist. "How many do you want?" "I want 12 tablets," says the old man, "and I want you to cut each of them into quarters for me." "Why do you want me to do that?" asks the pharmacist. "A quarter of a tablet won't do much for you." "Look, son," says the old man, "I'm over 90 years old. I don't need the tablets for sex. I just need them to make sure that when I go to the toilet it's sticking out far enough so it doesn't go all over my shoes."

An old man is telling his friend about his Viagra tablets. "It's the greatest thing I've ever known," he says. "It's the Fountain of Youth! It makes you feel like you're young again." "Can you get it over the counter in the chemist's?" asks his friend. "You can if you take six," replies the first.

An old man is at his dentist's. The dentist says, "I'm going to have to take one of your teeth out. I'll give you a shot of Novocain." The old man grabs the dentist's arm. "No! Please," he says, "I hate needles!" "OK," says the dentist. "Then I'll have to give you gas." "That's no good either," says the old man, "The gas always makes me sick for days." "In that case," says the dentist, "you'd better take this Viagra tablet." "Viagra?" says the old man. "Will that kill the pain?" "No," says the dentist, "but it will give you something to hang on to while I'm pulling your tooth."

An ageing spinster is sitting on a park bench one day all on her own. A rough looking man walks over and sits at the other end of the bench. After a few moments, the woman asks, "Are you a stranger here?" "I used to live here years ago," says the man. "Oh," says the woman. "So, where were you all these years?" "In prison," he says. "Oh," says the woman. "What did they put you in prison for?" And the rough man looks at her and very quietly says, "I got into a wild drunken rage one night and I killed my wife in the most violent terrible way imaginable." "Oh," says the woman. "So you're single then..."

An old man comes out of the newsagents and crosses over to the car parked opposite where a traffic warden is writing a ticket. "Oh come on!" says the old man. "I'm a pensioner. I can't afford to pay that, can I?" The traffic warden ignores him and continues writing the ticket. The old man becomes more abusive. "You fascist!" he says. "You slimy piece of I don't know what. You've got no heart. You pathetic, jumped-up stupid little man!" The traffic warden proceeds to write another ticket and then another as the old man keeps ranting at him about his lack of consideration. The car ends up with five tickets on the windscreen. "You should have spoken to him a bit more nicely," says a passer by to the old man, "and then he might have let you off." "I don't care," says the old man. "This isn't my car."

An old lady from a remote village in Cornwall goes to stay with her niece in Surrey. Nearby is a very well-known golf course. On the second afternoon of her visit, the elderly lady goes for a walk. Upon her return, the niece asks, "Well, Auntie, did you enjoy yourself?" "Oh, yes, indeed," says the old lady. "Before I had walked very far, I came to some beautiful rolling fields. There seemed to be a number of people wandering around them, mostly men. Some of them kept shouting at me in a very eccentric manner, but I took no notice. There were four men who followed me for some time, uttering curious excited barking sounds. Naturally, I ignored them, too. Oh, by the way," she says holding out her hands, "I found a number of these curious little round white balls, so I picked them all up and brought them home, hoping you could explain what they're all about."

An old man is telling his grandson about how he used to work in a blacksmith's when he was a boy. "Oh yes," says the old man, "I had to really toughen myself up to work in that place. Do you know I would stand at the back of my house, get a five-pound potato sack in my right hand and a 5-pound potato sack in my left hand, and then raise my arms up and extend them straight out from my sides. I'd then stand there holding them out like that for as long as I could. After a while I moved onto 10-pound potato sacks, then 20-pound potato sacks. Finally I was able to do it with a pair of 50-pound potato sacks." "Wow, granddad," says the little boy. "That must have been hard." "Oh yes," says the old man, "it was. And it was even worse when I started putting potatoes in the sacks."

Three old men are chatting about their ancestors and boasting about what they had done in the forces. The first one says, "My great grandfather was in the First World War trenches and survived." The second one says, "Well my great-grandfather was in the Boer War and he survived." Not to be outdone the third one says, "Well, if my great-grandfather was alive today he'd be internationally famous." "Really?" say the other two, leaning forward. "Why's that?" "Because he'd be 153 years old," says the third old man.

An old man goes to his doctor's and says he is worried about his failing sex drive and that his wife might stray if he is no longer able to satisfy her. "Hang on!" says the doctor to the old man. "How old are the pair of you?" "I'm 82," says the old man. "And my wife is 79." "OK," says the doctor. "And when did you notice this problem with your sex drive?" "Twice last night," says the old man, "and once again this morning."

An old man asks his similarly aged neighbour if he would mind popping into town to the post office to see if a package he is expecting has turned up yet. His old neighbour says he was going into town anyway to get his groceries. So off he totters, into the town. The old man sits watching for several hours until eventually his elderly neighbour re-appears, slowly plodding all the way back down the street again. "So?" says the old man to his neighbour. "Was my package there?" "Oh yes," says the neighbour. "It's there all right."

A little old lady is in court for stealing a tin of peaches after absentmindedly popping them into her bag rather than her trolley. Under the circumstances the judge decides to be lenient and asks her how many peaches there were in the tin. "There were three peaches," she replies. "Very well then," says the judge, "in that case I sentence you to three days in prison." Just then her husband pipes up and says, "She stole a tin of peas as well!"

An elderly lady calls 999 on her mobile phone. In a panic she calls for the police to come quickly, because her car has been broken into and a number of items have been stolen. "What exactly has been taken, madam?" asks the operator at the other end of the line. "Oh it's terrible, officer," says the old lady. "They've taken my car stereo. They've taken the steering wheel, the gear stick, the brake pedal and even the accelerator!" "My goodness," says the operator, "I've never heard of anything like this before. I'm sending someone out straightaway." A few minutes later the operator gets a call from the policeman attending the scene. "Case solved!" says the policeman. "The stupid old woman climbed into the back seat by mistake."

An elderly gentleman came home one night to find a homeless girl of about 18 ransacking his house. He grabbed her by the arm and was just about to call the police when the girl dropped down on her knees and begged him, "Please don't call the police! I'm in too much trouble already. In fact, if you don't call the police, I'll let you make love to me and do all the things you've ever wanted to do!" The old man thinks about this for a minute and finally yields to temptation. Soon the pair are in bed together, but despite the old man's very best efforts he finds he no longer has what it takes. Finally he gives up. He rolls over exhausted and reaches for the phone. "I'm sorry, young lady... but it's no use," he gasps. "It looks like I'm going to have to call the police after all."

A very old man is lying on his deathbed. He summons his lawyer and tells him to make some last-minute changes to his will. "I wish to leave everything I own, all stocks, bonds, property, art and money to my nagging, spiteful, ungrateful, mean-spirited wife. However, there is one stipulation." "And that is?" asks the lawyer. "In order to inherit," says the old man, "she must marry within six months of my death." "That's a bit of an odd request," says the lawyer. "Why do you want to do that?"

"Because," says the old man, "I want someone to be sorry I died."

The family of a rich old man gathers to hear his will being read. The solicitor solemnly opens the document and reads, "The last will and testament of John Smith. Being of sound mind, I therefore spent all my money."

A woman goes to the undertakers to see her late husband's body just before his burial. When she gets there she is shocked to find him dressed in a grey suit. "Oh no," she says. "I can't have him buried in a grey suit. He couldn't stand grey. He always said he wanted to be buried in a black suit." "I'm sorry, I can't do anything about it now, madam," says the undertaker. "It's too late. The funeral is going to begin in a few minutes." "But I insist!" shouts the woman, breaking into tears. "All right, madam," says the undertaker. "Calm down. I'll see what I can do." The undertaker pushes the trolley with the man's body out into the back room. A few moments later an assistant pushes the trolley back in with the woman's husband now dressed in a black suit. "My goodness that was quick!" says the undertaker under his breath. "How did you do it?" "Oh it wasn't too hard," says the assistant. "Luckily we had a bloke out there already dressed in a black suit so we just swapped the heads over."

An old man lying on his deathbed summons his doctor, his lawyer and his priest. He hands out three separate envelopes to them. Each of the envelopes contains £30,000. "Gentlemen," he tells them solemnly, "They say you can't take it with you, but I am going to try. When they lower my coffin into my grave I want each of you to throw in these envelopes I have just given you." After the funeral the doctor confesses to the other two, "I've got to be straight with you. My health practice desperately needed some money to build a new clinic, so I kept £20,000 and just threw in £10,000." The priest also confesses, "The church is in desperate need of renovation. So I'm afraid I kept £10,000 and just threw in £20,000." The lawyer stands shaking his head in disgust. "I can't believe you two," he says. "Am I the only one of us who was decent enough to carry out the old man's dying wishes?" "So you threw in the entire £30,000!" say the doctor and the priest in astonishment. "Yes," says the lawyer. "Well... I threw in a cheque for the full amount."

An old lady in London decides to draw up her will and make her last requests. She tells her solicitor she is leaving her fortune to her daughters, but with two important conditions. Firstly, she says she wants to be cremated, and secondly, she wants her ashes scattered over the first floor of Harrods department store. "Harrods!" says the solicitor. "Why Harrods?" "Well," says the old lady, "at least that way I'll be sure my daughters will visit my final resting place each week."

Winston, an old Scotsman is dying and he calls for his best friend Rory to come to his bedside and listen to his dying wish. "Rory," whispers old Winston, his breath almost spent, "Under my bed you'll find a bottle of the world's finest single malt. I've been saving it for this moment. When you come to my funeral would ye do me the great service of pouring the whiskey over my grave?" "Aye, of course I will, my friend," replies Rory, and then adds, "But would you mind terribly if I pass it through my bladder first?"

Two old men are talking. "I reckon death must be the best part of life," says one. "Why's that?" asks the other. "Because," says the first, "It always gets saved till last."

Two recently bereaved women are chatting at a support group and one says, "Don't talk to me about solicitors, I've had so much trouble sorting out my late husband's will that I sometimes wish he hadn't died."

Doris is dying, and calls in her husband. "Arthur," she says, "When you go to the church for my funeral I want you to promise that you'll sit next to my mother and keep her company." "Oh no," says Arthur, "Do I have to? You know I can't stand the woman, and she makes no secret of the fact that she can't stand me." "But Arthur," protested the woman, "It's my dying wish. Can't you make an effort just for me?" "Oh all right," says Arthur, "But I want you to know this is going to completely ruin the whole day for me."

Two old ladies bump into each other at the supermarket. "Hello, dear. How are you?" asks the first. "Oh I'm fine," says the second. "And what about your husband?" asks the first. "Oh, didn't you hear?" says the second. "He died two weeks ago. He went out in the garden to dig up a cabbage for dinner, had a massive heart attack and fell over in the compost heap, stone dead." "Oh my goodness!" says the first old lady.

"How absolutely terrible for you. What did you do?" "Well," says the second, "luckily I managed to find a tin of sweetcorn in the cupboard, so I had that instead."

An old couple wake up one morning and the old man leans over to kiss his wife on the cheek. "No!" squeals his wife, "Don't touch me! I think I've died!" "What are you talking about, woman?" says the old man. "How can you have died when you're sitting up in bed with me." "I don't know," says the old woman, "but I think I've definitely died in my sleep." "Well, what makes you think that?" says the man. "Because," says the old woman, "I've just woken up and nothing's hurting."

Joe tells his friend Pete, "My granddad died last night." "Oh no," says Pete. "Yes," says Joe, "He was working late in the whiskey distillery, he had to climb up to check in one of the vats, but being a bit doddery on his legs now he lost his balance and fell in." "Oh my goodness!" says Pete. "So what happened? Did he drown?" "Yes. After eight hours," says Joe. "Eight hours!" says Pete. "Why so long?" "Well it would have been quicker," says Joe, "but he had to get out three times to go to the toilet."

Roger and Catherine are talking one day and the subject turns to death. "What would you do if I died before you?" asks Roger. "Oh, I don't know really," says Catherine. "I suppose thinking about it, I'd have to sell this place, because it would be far too big for me, and then I'd get in touch with my best friend Julie and move in with her now that her husband's gone. What about you?" "Hmm," says Roger, "Probably exactly the same as you."

Gertrude and Hilda are sitting in the bingo hall between games and looking out of the window. As they do so a funeral procession goes by and the name of the deceased, 'Albert', is spelt out in flowers in the back of the hearse. Gertrude sniffs loudly and gets a hanky out of her handbag. Hilda says, "Oh you old softie!" "I can't help it," says Gertrude. "After all, he was a good husband to me."

Granddad was in hospital and one of his teenage grandchildren was looking after the cat while grandma was at work. One day the teenager announced that the cat had died. "My poor old Polly?" said granddad, "You could have broken it to me gently." "How?" asked the teenager. "You could have said Polly was playing on the roof, then she slipped and hurt herself, and you took her to the vet and he couldn't save her." "I see," said the teenager, "Sorry, Granddad." A week later the teenager went to visit granddad in hospital. "Hello," said Granddad, "How's Grandma?" "Well," said the teenager, "She was playing on the roof..."

A funeral service is being held for a woman who has just passed away. At the end of the service, the pall bearers are carrying the coffin out when they accidentally bump into a wall, jarring the casket. They hear a faint moan! They open the lid of the coffin and are amazed to discover that the woman is still alive after all. She lives for another ten years before passing on. Once again, a funeral service is held and, at the end of it, the pall bearers pick up the coffin, and start carrying it out of the church. As

they carry the coffin towards the door,
the husband cries out: "This time will
you watch out for that bloody wall!"

At an old man's funeral, the vicar talks at some length about the good life of the dearly departed, what a pillar of the community he has been, what a loving husband and kind father, and how he will be sadly missed by all his poor family. Listening to this, the old man's widow looks increasingly concerned. "Are you all right, Mum?" asks her son, fearing she is about to break down with emotion. "I'm fine," says the old lady, "but could you just go and have a quick look to make sure we've got the right person in the coffin. I'm not sure he can be talking about your father."

Fred tells Ethel, "Do you know, my granddad knew the exact date and the exact time that he would die." "That's uncanny," says Ethel. "Was he psychic then?" "No," says Fred. "The judge told him."

In the churchyard the undertaker is standing next to the grieving widow. The old woman is crying uncontrollably and so the undertaker tries to cheer her up by starting a conversation. "How old was your husband then?" he asks. "My Bert was 97," replies the widow. "Only a few months older than I am." "Oh dear. Is that so?" says the undertaker. "So really when you think about it, it's hardly worth you going home is it?"

A widower who never paid any attention to his wife while she was alive now found himself missing her desperately. He went to a psychic to see if he could contact her. Suddenly the man heard the unmistakable voice of his dearly departed wife. "Dearest!" he cried. "Is that you?" "Yes, my husband," she replied. "Are you happy?" "Yes, my husband." "Happier than you were with me?" "Oh yes, my husband, I am." "Wow," he said. "So Heaven must be an amazing place!" "I'm not in Heaven, dear," said his wife.

A little old lady goes to a medium to help her contact her dead husband. "He's with me now, dear," says the medium, "Is there anything you want to ask him?" "Well," says the old lady, "just ask him if there's anything he needs." "He says he'd like a packet of cigarettes," says the medium. "OK," says the little old lady. "Did he say where I should send them to?" "No," replies the medium. "But he did say that where he is he won't be needing a lighter."

An old married couple have an accident in their car and go straight up to Heaven. When they get there they look round in amazement at the wonder and tranquillity of the place. "Oh my!" says the wife. "It's so beautiful and peaceful, it's even better than I imagined." The husband hasn't said a word since they got there, so she turns to him and says, "What's the matter, Henry, don't you like it?" "Like it?" replies the husband. "It's fantastic! And if it hadn't been for you and your health foods I could've been up here years ago!"

A lawyer and the Pope died at the same time and both went to Heaven. They were met at the Pearly Gates by St Peter who conducted them to their rooms. The Pope's room was spartan, with a bare floor, an army bunk for a bed and a single bulb for light. They came to the lawyer's room. It was huge, with wall-to-wall carpeting, king-sized water bed, indirect lighting, colour TV, stereo, jacuzzi and a fully stocked bar. The lawyer said, "There must be a mistake. This must be the Pope's room!"

St Peter said, "There's no mistake. This is your room. We have lots of Popes, but you're our very first lawyer!"

An old man says to his friend, "You know, even though I'm old, I've definitely still got it." "Oh yes," says his friend. "Yes," says the old man. "The problem is nobody wants it any more."

After losing her husband a woman decides to go to a medium to try and contact him. After a while the medium says she thinks the husband is with them. "How are you?" the widow asks. "I'm fine," says the husband. "In fact, I'm great. I'm in a lovely green field surrounded by cows." "Oh," says the widow, rather surprised. "And some of them are very attractive," says the husband. "Really?" says the widow. "And are there angels there?" "No, just cows," says the husband. "I think I'm going to enjoy myself." "Well, that's good I suppose," says the widow. "But why do you keep going on about cows?" "Didn't I tell you?" says the husband. "I'm on a farm at Ilkley Moor – I've come back as a bull!"

A woman goes on holiday to South Africa. Her husband is meeting her there the following day. When she has checked in, she sends her husband an e-mail, but sends it to the wrong address. The next day the grieving widower of a recently deceased Sunday school teacher checks his e-mail, shouts out in horror and drops dead from a heart attack. Afterwards his cleaner finds a disturbing message on his computer screen: "Darling, Just got checked in. Everything ready for your arrival tomorrow. Your loving wife. P.S. Wow it's really hot down here."

St Peter is guarding the Pearly Gates when he hears a knock at the door. He goes to answer it, but there's nobody there. A few minutes later there's another knock. Again he goes to answer it, but once more there's nobody there. After another few minutes there's yet another knock at the door and this time there's an old man standing there. "What's your game?" asks St Peter. "Have you been playing 'knock down ginger' on my door?" "No," says the man. "The doctors were trying to resuscitate me."

A man dies and his wife phones the local paper to arrange for his obituary to be printed. She is put through to the correct department and tells them she doesn't have much money, so she just wants the obituary to say, 'Alf is dead'. "That's quite short," says the man at the newspaper office, "but if you're worrying about the cost, don't forget you're entitled to have up to six words for the same price." "In that case," says the woman, "make it, 'Alf is dead: Toyota for sale'."

A woman is at the solicitor's listening to the reading of her late husband's will. She is shocked and outraged to find that he has left all his money to another woman, so she stomps off to the graveyard, where the man from the undertaker's has just laid his headstone reading 'Rest in Peace'. Despite her protests the undertaker says it's too late to change the inscription. "All right then," she says. "After 'Rest in Peace' just add 'For the Time Being'."

An old lady commissions an artist to paint her portrait. He arrives to find her dripping in very expensive-looking jewellery: a diamond necklace, diamond earrings and a diamond tiara. "Wow!" says the artist. "That must be worth an absolute fortune, if you don't mind me saying." "Well, it is," replies the old lady, "but I've only rented it." "Oh, I see," says the artist, "You just want it to look good for the portrait?" "No," says the old lady, "but when I die my husband will probably remarry and I want the little gold-digger to go mad looking for the jewellery."

An elderly couple are discussing their funeral arrangements one day and the wife says to the husband, "So, Bert, when you die would you like to be buried or cremated?" "I don't know," replies her husband. "Surprise me!"

Three old men are talking about what their grandchildren might be saying about them in 50 years' time. "I would like my grandchildren to say, 'He was successful in business'," says the first old man. "Fifty years from now," says the second, "I want them to say, 'He was a loyal family man'." Turning to the third old man, the first gent asks, "So what do you want them to say about you in 50 years?" "Me?" says the third old man. "I want them all to say, 'My! He looks good for his age!'"

An old lady tells her friend, "My husband died the other day." "Oh dear," says her friend. "What of?" "The doctors aren't sure," says the old lady, "but they don't think it was anything serious."

A 90-year-old man has been married four times, but appears at his doctor's to announce that he is getting married again, to a highly sexed 18-year-old girl. "Are you mad?" says the doctor. "You realize that if you start having frequent sex again it could prove fatal." "Ah well," says the old man, "if she dies, she dies."